Walton arr. Lambert

Façade Suite 1

for piano duet

(an arrangement of the orchestral suite)

Contents:

Polka, *Valse*, *Swiss Jodelling Song*, *Tango-Pasodoblé*, and *Tarantella Sevillana*.

Music Department
OXFORD UNIVERSITY PRESS
Oxford and New York

FAÇADE
SUITE FOR ORCHESTRA
(after poems by EDITH SITWELL)

I. POLKA

**Arranged for four hands by
CONSTANT LAMBERT**

WILLIAM WALTON

Printed in Great Britain

OXFORD UNIVERSITY PRESS, MUSIC DEPARTMENT, 44 CONDUIT STREET, LONDON, W.1

2

4

5

II. VALSE

9

III. SWISS JODELLING SONG

Lento con Tristezza

18

20

*IV. TANGO - PASODOBLÉ

* In the *Tango* 'I do like to be beside the seaside' is used by arrangement with Messrs. B. Feldman & Co.

22

23

24

V. TARANTELLA SEVILLANA

27

28

OXFORD UNIVERSITY PRESS